ICONS

ARIANA GRANDE

BY KATHLEEN CONNORS

Enslow PUBLISHING

Please visit our website, www.enslow.com.
For a free color catalog of all our high-quality books, call toll free 1-800-398-2504 or fax 1-877-980-4454.

Library of Congress Cataloging-in-Publication Data

Names: Connors, Kathleen, author.
Title: Ariana Grande / Kathleen Connors.
Description: Buffalo, New York : Enslow Publishing, 2026. | Series: Icons | Includes index.
Identifiers: LCCN 2024061904 (print) | LCCN 2024061905 (ebook) | ISBN 9781978544499 (library binding) | ISBN 9781978544482 (paperback) | ISBN 9781978544505 (ebook)
Subjects: LCSH: Grande, Ariana--Juvenile literature. | Singers--United States--Biography--Juvenile literature. | LCGFT: Biographies.
Classification: LCC ML3930.G724 C66 2026 (print) | LCC ML3930.G724 (ebook) | DDC 782.42164092 [B]--dc23/eng/20241230
LC record available at https://lccn.loc.gov/2024061904
LC ebook record available at https://lccn.loc.gov/2024061905

Published in 2026 by
Enslow Publishing
2544 Clinton Street
Buffalo, NY 14224

Designer: Tanya Dellaccio Keeney
Editor: Kristen Rajczak Nelson

Photo credits: Cover Sipa USA/Alamy Images; p. 4 Featureflash Photo Agency/Shutterstock.com; pp. 5, 20 Image Press Agency/Alamy Images; pp. 7, 17 WENN Rights Ltd/Alamy Images; p. 9 PHOTOlink/Alamy Images; p. 11 imageBROKER.com GmbH & Co. KG/Alamy Images; pp. 13, 14, 29 Everett Collection Inc/Alamy Images; p. 15 Jamie Lamor Thompson/Shutterstock.com; p. 16 camerongtfc / Stockimo/Alamy Images; p. 19 Erik Pendzich/Alamy Images; pp. 21, 27 Album/Alamy Images; p. 23 Invision/AP Images; p. 25 Doug Peters/Alamy Images.

Printed in the United States of America

CPSIA compliance information: Batch #CSENS26: For further information contact Enslow Publishing, at 1-800-398-2504.

Contents

Words in the glossary appear in **bold** the first time they are used in the text.

Meet Ariana Grande

Ariana Grande was born on June 26, 1993. She grew up in Boca Raton, Florida. Her mom, Joan Grande, and her dad, Ed Butera, broke up with she was still a kid. She has a brother named Frankie.

Frankie Grande

ICONIC!

Ariana grew up listening to Mariah Carey, Whitney Houston, Madonna, and other female superstars with her mom and brother.

Broadway Bound

Ariana started singing when she was young. She **performed** with a local children's theater too. Then, in 2008, Ariana landed a part on Broadway! She was just 15 when she performed in the show *13*.

ICONIC!

Ariana says she learned how to sing well partly by trying to sound like singer Céline Dion.

Taking on TV

Not long after *13* closed, Ariana was cast in a Nickelodeon show, *Victorious*. She played Cat Valentine, a girl who goes to a performing arts school. It started airing in 2010. *Victorious* put Ariana in the spotlight!

ICONIC!

Victorious ended in 2013. Ariana then starred as Cat again in the show *Sam & Cat*.

Record Deal

Ariana liked acting but wanted to make music most of all. She signed with Republic Records in 2011. She put out the song "Put Your Hearts Up." But later, she said the "bubblegum pop" sound of the song wasn't for her.

ICONIC!

Ariana has a four-octave singing range. That means she can sing all the notes in four octaves well.

102.7
102.7

Ariana got to show the R&B music she wanted to make on her first album *Yours Truly*. It **debuted** at number one in August 2013! In 2014, Ariana put out *My Everything*. This album was a bit more pop. The first single, "Problem," was an instant hit.

ICONIC!

Ariana told Rolling Stone *in 2014 that acting is fun "but music has always been first and foremost with me."*

Ariana had a string of hit songs when *Dangerous Woman* came out in 2016, including "Into You," "Dangerous Woman," and "Side to Side." The album was **nominated** for best pop vocal album at the Grammy **Awards**.

ICONIC!

Ariana is known for her ***impressions*** *of other famous people. She wowed fans—and gained new ones—when she hosted* Saturday Night Live *for the first time in 2016.*

Manchester Bombing

On the Dangerous Woman Tour in 2017, Ariana played a sold-out concert in Manchester, United Kingdom. A bomb went off after the concert, killing 20 people. Ariana was **devastated**. She organized the One Love Manchester concert to help raise money for those who had been hurt.

ICONIC!

Ariana now speaks out about gun control. She performed at the March for Our Lives in 2018, which was put on after a school shooting in Parkland, Florida.

Getting the Grammys

Ariana won best pop vocal album at the Grammy Awards for *Sweetener*, which came out in 2018. It hit number one on the *Billboard* 200 chart too! In 2019, Ariana put out *thank u, next*. The **lyrics** were very personal, and fans really connected with them.

ICONIC!

At one point in 2019, Ariana had the number one, number two, and number three songs on the Billboard *Hot 100 chart!*

Finally, Ariana was making music that sounded just how she wanted it to. She followed up the success of *thank u, next* with *Positions* in 2020. The next year she won her second Grammy Award for a song with Lady Gaga called "Rain on Me."

ICONIC!

Ariana had a few acting roles while she put out her many albums. One special part was Penny Pingleton in the 2016 Hairspray Live!

Featuring...

Since Ariana started recording music, she has worked with other music artists. She has had success with songs featuring the Weeknd, Nicki Minaj, Doja Cat, Charli XCX, and more. The song "Stuck With U," which Ariana recorded with Justin Bieber, debuted at number one in May 2020.

ICONIC!

Ariana loves dogs and owns many! She has taken in most of them from animal shelters.

Ariana got married in 2021. By 2024, that marriage had ended. She put out *eternal sunshine*, which was about the breakup. Ariana wrote and **produced** the album. She wrote the lyrics to "yes, and?" and "eternal sunshine," among others, with no co-writers.

ICONIC!

Ariana has written many of her own songs as well as songs for other artists, including co-writing "Ice Cream" by BLACKPINK.

The Good Witch

In 2021, Ariana took on a dream role: Glinda in the movie of the musical *Wicked*. The first part came out in 2024 and the second part in 2025. Ariana got to show off her high notes as well as how funny she is in the part.

ICONIC!

When she sang for Wicked's director Jon M. Chu, Ariana sang both Glinda songs and those sung by Elphaba, the "wicked" witch in the movie. They both knew she should be Glinda though!

What an Icon!

With her range, both as an actor and singer, Ariana is truly an icon. She's also a businesswoman! Ariana has a line of fragrances, or perfumes, some of which are named after songs. She also founded r.e.m. beauty! What else will she accomplish?

ICONIC!

Ariana was nominated for a Golden Globe and an Academy Award for playing Glinda.

Timeline

1993	Ariana Grande is born.
2008	She starts performing in 13 on Broadway.
2010	She starts playing Cat Valentine on Victorious.
2011	She signs a deal with Republic Records. Her first song comes out.
2013	Victorious ends. Ariana plays Cat again on Sam & Cat. Yours Truly comes out.
2014	My Everything comes out.
2016	Dangerous Woman comes out.
2017	A bombing occurs after a show on the Dangerous Woman Tour.
2018	Sweetener comes out.
2019	Ariana wins her first Grammy Award for Sweetener. Thank u, next comes out.
2020	Positions comes out.
2021	Ariana wins another Grammy Award.
2024	Eternal sunshine comes out. Ariana first stars in Wicked.

For More Information

BOOKS

Anderson, Kirsten. *Who Is Ariana Grande?*. New York, NY: Penguin Workshop, 2024.

Rose, Rachel. *Ariana Grande: Pop Vocal Powerhouse*. Minneapolis, MN: Lerner Publications, 2025.

WEBSITE

Ariana Grande
https://www.arianagrande.com
Keep up with Ariana on her website.

Ariana Grande - IMDb
https://www.imdb.com/name/nm3812858/
Look back on Ariana's career on the Internet Movie Database.

Publisher's note to educators and parents: Our editors have carefully reviewed these websites to ensure that they are suitable for students. Many websites change frequently, however, and we cannot guarantee that a site's future contents will continue to meet our high standards of quality and educational value. Be advised that students should be closely supervised whenever they access the internet.

Glossary

award: A prize.

debut: To appear to the public for the first time.

devastated: Very upset.

impression: A copy of the way someone acts and talks.

lyrics: The words to a song.

nominate: To suggest someone for an honor.

octave: The notes from one end of a musical scale to another.

perform: To play music or sing.

produce: To organize, supervise, and help make music.

Index